# Super Suppers and Desserts!

Written by
**Kids Cooking Club**®

Illustrated by
**Yancey Labat**

Scholastic Inc.

New York   Toronto   London   Auckland   Sydney   Mexico City   New Delhi   Hong Kong   Buenos Aires

Designed by Peggy Gardner

ISBN 0-439-83225-X

12 11 10 9 8 7 6 5 4 3 2     7 8 9 10/0

Printed in China

First Scholastic printing, May 2006

# Sit Right Down for a Super Supper (Complete With Dessert)!

Ever wonder what's for supper? Take the guesswork out by taking charge! That's right! YOU be the one who makes a super supper tonight!

Use this great new cookbook to make meals with color, style, and crunch, as well as desserts that are a sweet treat to the very end. Let an adult assist you in taking over the kitchen. Your family will be wowed by what you've made with the help of Kids Cooking Club!

# The Supper Rules

◆ **Read completely:** read recipes all the way through before starting. Several recipes require extra time for ingredients to marinate, set, or refrigerate.

◆ **Dress ready:** wear an apron, short sleeves, and tie back long hair.

◆ **Start clean:** wash hands, start with clean tools and work area.

◆ **Be prepared:** get out all ingredients and tools needed for the recipe before starting.

◆ **Clean up:** put things away along the way.

◆ **Be safe:** know where and how to use the fire extinguisher in your kitchen.

◆ **Have fun:** but don't play roughhouse in the kitchen.

◆ **Be supervised:** have an adult with you at all times in the kitchen. Grown up supervision is required when using the barbeque, stove, oven, microwave, appliances, and knives.

## NOTE TO GROWN-UPS:

All of the recipes in this book are designed for adult supervision **at all times**. Kids should never be left alone in the kitchen. There are many steps that grown-ups need to handle or supervise including, but not limited to, using a barbeque, stove, microwave, and oven, handling hot pans, working with sharp knives, operating appliances, and ensuring that the barbeque, oven, and stove are turned off after use.

 We have placed this icon next to those steps that will require your help.

## PLAN AHEAD!

Please note that several recipes require extra time for ingredients to marinate or set in the refrigerator or freezer. We also feature two great crock-pot recipes to start in the morning. Plan accordingly so kids don't get discouraged once they start a recipe and cannot finish it right away. Also have the ingredients ready to put in the crock-pot come morning.

 **PLAN AHEAD!** We have placed this icon next to those recipes.

# The Supper Tools:

Along with the basics, here are different tools you will use in this cookbook:

Cheese grater: grating cheese, zesting, and mincing.

Crock-pot: every busy family should have one in their dinner arsenal.

 Cutting board: there's lots to chop and cut at dinner. Be sure to wash off well with soap after contact with raw meats.

Grill grid/grate: works well for grilled veggies.

 Knives: a small paring knife for cutting, serrated knife for breads.

Mini pie pans: (5-inch diameter) for pot pies.

**Pie server:** for slicing and serving pie and desserts.

**Potato Masher:** for mashing potatoes, vegetables, and fruits.

**Salad tongs:** for tossing and serving salad.

**Skewers:** (bamboo or metal) to spear kebabs.

**Slotted spoon:** great for mixing and stirring.

**Soup ladle:** for serving soup, ladling ingredients into piecrusts.

**Large skillet:** great for making fried rice.

# Super Supper Terms:

Here are some familiar and new terms that you will see often in this cookbook:

**Bouillon cubes:** used in soup and broths, found in soup section of grocery store.

**Broil:** to cook directly under the heat source (cooks very fast).

**Brown:** to cook food until it turns a light brown color on the outer surface.

**Diced:** to cut into small even-sized pieces.

**Divided:** means an ingredient is used more than once in the recipe.

**Finely chopped:** to cut into very small pieces.

**Grated:** cheese, fruit, or vegetables rubbed on a box grater to create fine particles.

**Marinate:** to soak in a sauce. The longer, the more flavor is absorbed.

Make this by simply following
the steps. It's easy as 1-2-3!

TOOLS:

- Measuring
  cups & spoons
- Knife &
  cutting board
- Large skillet
- Slotted spoon
- Colander
- Can opener

INGREDIENTS:

1 pound ground meat
1 cup chopped onion
1 teaspoon minced garlic
¼ teaspoon black pepper
1 15.5-ounce can beef broth
4 cups water
1 beef bouillon cube
1½ teaspoons Italian seasoning
1 16-ounce can whole chopped
  tomatoes
1 8-ounce can of kidney beans,
  undrained
1½ cups sliced carrots

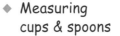

1 cup frozen green beans
1 cup frozen lima beans
1 cup dried alphabet pasta

## STEPS:

1. Put ground meat, prepared onion, garlic, and pepper in skillet on medium-high heat. Stir to break up meat into pieces and cook until meat is browned all the way through. Drain meat in colander and return to skillet.

2. Add the remaining ingredients EXCEPT ABC pasta and cook over medium heat for about 20 minutes to let ingredients blend.

3. Add ABC pasta and cook until tender.

## SERVING SUGGESTIONS:

- ❖ Top with fresh Parmesan and chopped basil
- ❖ Add a side of garlic breadsticks as soup dippers
- ❖ Serve in mugs on a cold day

S T U V W X Y Z A B C D E F G H I J

# Cheesy, Crunchy, Goldfish Chowder

No, we don't use real goldfish in this heart-warming chowder, just our favorite little crackers to make it extra crunchy.

SERVES 4

**TOOLS:**
- Measuring cups
- Knife & cutting board
- Large soup pot
- Slotted spoon
- Can opener
- Soup ladle
- Serving bowls

**INGREDIENTS:**

4 cups water

2 chicken bouillon cubes

2 cups diced potatoes
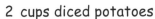
1 cup diced onion

1 bunch fresh broccoli, chopped
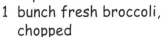
2 10.5-ounce cans of cream of chicken soup
1 pound cheddar cheese, grated
Goldfish crackers, to taste

## STEPS:

1. Put water, bouillon cubes, prepared potatoes, onion, and broccoli in soup pot.
2. Cook over medium heat, stirring occasionally, for about 30 minutes.
3. Add cream of chicken soup and grated cheese and let simmer for 15 minutes.
4. Ladle into serving bowls and top each with a handful of goldfish crackers.

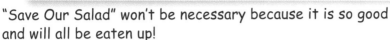

# SOS (Strawberries Over Spinach)

SERVES 4

"Save Our Salad" won't be necessary because it is so good and will all be eaten up!

## INGREDIENTS FOR DRESSING:

- 2 tablespoons sesame seeds
- 1 tablespoon poppy seeds
- ½ cup sugar
- ½ cup olive oil
- ¼ cup red or white wine vinegar
- ¼ teaspoon paprika
- ¼ teaspoon Worcestershire sauce
- 1 tablespoon minced onion

## INGREDIENTS FOR SALAD:

- 10-ounces fresh spinach, rinsed, dried and torn into bite-sized pieces
- ½ cup pecans
- 1 quart strawberries, washed and sliced

## ⏰ PLAN AHEAD!

1. In mixing bowl, whisk together the sesame seeds, poppy seeds, sugar, olive oil, vinegar, paprika, Worcestershire sauce, and onion. Cover, and chill for one hour.

2. Put the torn spinach leaves in a salad bowl. Sprinkle the pecans and sliced strawberries on top of spinach. Drizzle on the dressing, toss and refrigerate for 10 to 15 minutes before serving.

### TOOLS:

◆ Measuring spoons & cups
◆ Mixing bowl with top or foil cover
◆ Whisk
◆ Knife & cutting board
◆ Salad bowl & tongs

# Corn Cobber Salad

Eat your salad and vegetables at once with this great recipe.

## INGREDIENTS:

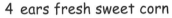

- 4 ears fresh sweet corn
- 4 cups romaine lettuce, torn in bite-sized pieces
- 3 cups cooked chicken, cut in strips
- 4 slices bacon, cooked and crumbled
- 2 green onion stalks, thinly sliced
- 1 bottle of Ranch dressing

**SERVES 4**

## TOOLS:

- ◆ Soup pot
- ◆ Knife & cutting board
- ◆ Colander
- ◆ Large measuring cup
- ◆ 4 fancy serving plates

## Make the corn on the cob:

1. Fill soup pot with water to about ¾-full and bring to boil.
2. Remove husks from corn. Cut each ear into thirds and put into boiling water.
3. Cook until tender, about 4 minutes, then drain and set aside.

## Make the salad:

On each of the four fancy serving plates evenly arrange the salad as follows with the other prepared ingredients:

- ❖ Torn Romaine lettuce leaves
- ❖ Cooked chicken strips
- ❖ Cooked corn on the cob pieces
- ❖ Crumbled bacon and green onion slices
- ❖ A drizzle of Ranch dressing to taste

# MVP Casserole

This recipe might be the "most-valuable-player" in the cookbook because it's really a three-course dinner (Meat, Vegetables, and Potatoes) wrapped up in one great dish!

## Tools:

- Measuring cups & spoons
- Skillet
- Spoon
- Colander
- Fork
- 9 x 13-inch baking dish

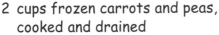

## Ingredients:

Serves 6

- 4 cup mashed potatoes*
- 2 cups frozen carrots and peas, cooked and drained
- 1 tablespoon oil
- 1 large onion, chopped
- 1 pound ground beef
- 2 beef bouillon cubes
- 1½ cups water, divided
- 2 tablespoons cornstarch
- 1 cup cheddar cheese, grated

*make homemade from about 2 pounds of favorite potatoes or use a 20-ounce package of pre-made refrigerated mashed potatoes found at the grocery store

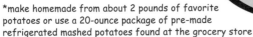

## STEPS:

1. Preheat oven to 375°F.

2. Prepare mashed potatoes. Either make them fresh or follow the package instructions if you are using pre-made. Also prepare frozen carrots and peas per package instructions.

3. Put oil and chopped onion in skillet and lightly sauté until soft. Add ground beef and break into small pieces as you brown the meat. Put meat and onions in colander to drain out the fat and put back in skillet.

4. Break up bouillon cubes and sprinkle on meat. Add 1 cup of the water, add cooked carrots and peas, and let simmer for 10 minutes.

5. Use a fork to mix the cornstarch with the remaining ½ cup of water. Add to meat and vegetable mixture to thicken it. Cook for about 2 minutes and then transfer to baking dish.

6. Spread mashed potatoes on top, then sprinkle with grated cheese. Bake for 20 minutes or until potatoes are heated through and lightly browned on top.

# Pork Chops & Applesauce

This is a favorite "comfort" dish.

**SERVES 4**

## INGREDIENTS:

1 tablespoon oil
4 pork chops
4 cups applesauce
½ cup apple juice

1 teaspoon cinnamon-sugar mixture
¼ teaspoon nutmeg

## TOOLS:

- Skillet
- Spatula
- 9-inch square baking dish
- Measuring cups & spoons
- Mixing bowl

## STEPS:

1. Preheat oven to 350°F.
2. Put oil in skillet and lightly brown both sides of the pork chops, 3 minutes on each side. Put browned pork chops in baking dish.
3. Mix together applesauce, apple juice, cinnamon/sugar, and nutmeg in mixing bowl.
4. Spoon half of the applesauce mixture over pork chops and bake for 20 minutes. Remove from oven, turn pork chops over, add remaining applesauce mixture, and bake for another 20 minutes until done.

# Make Your Own Applesauce

## INGREDIENTS:

4 Granny Smith apples
3 tablespoons unsalted butter
$\frac{1}{4}$ cup sugar
Cinnamon

## TOOLS:

- Vegetable peeler
- Knife
- Saucepan with lid
- Measuring cups
- Large spoon

## STEPS:

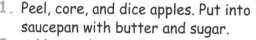

1. Peel, core, and dice apples. Put into saucepan with butter and sugar.
2. Add enough water to just cover the apples and put on lid. Cook over medium heat until apples are chunky—but tender—and the water has turned into a light syrup, about 30 minutes.
3. Check it every so often. If water cooks away before apples are done, add a little more so the pan doesn't dry out. Serve with cinnamon sprinkled on top.

# Burger Be Mine!

When it comes to hamburgers, everyone has a unique idea about what toppings are best! Here are some ideas, but be sure to have your burger your way!

## Start With the Basic Burger

### INGREDIENTS:

- 1 pound ground beef or turkey
- 6 tablespoons dry breadcrumbs
- 1 teaspoon Worcestershire sauce
- Salt & pepper to taste
- Hamburger buns

## STEPS:

1. Put ground meat, breadcrumbs, Worcestershire sauce, salt, and pepper into mixing bowl and use your clean hands to combine.

2. Check the "Mix-In" list (page 22) to stylize your burger before cooking. If you choose any of the mix-ins, add now and then form into 4-6 evenly sized patties.

3. Grill, broil, or fry burgers making sure to flip them at least once. Cook about 8 minutes for medium and 10 minutes for well-done. Please note that the extra goodies in the meat may require longer cooking time, so have an adult check the inside to be sure it is not pink.

4. Check the "Top-With" list (below) to make it special after it's cooked. Serve on hamburger buns.

TOOLS:
- Measuring spoons
- Mixing bowl
- Platter
- Spatula

MAKES 4-6 BURGERS SIZED TO LIKING

## —— Mix-in* any of the following before cooking: ——

**All-American style:** diced hot dogs and shredded cheddar cheese

**Italian style:** fresh Parmesan, tomato sauce, and Italian seasoning

**Santa Fe style:** salsa, tortilla chips, green onions, and guacamole

**Greek style:** feta cheese, diced Kalamata olives, and red onions

**Popeye style:** chopped fresh spinach leaves and ricotta cheese

**Veggie style:** diced mushrooms, bell peppers, onions, and yellow squash

## —— Top-with any of the following after cooking: ——

**Cowboy style:** cooked chili, diced onions, and melted cheddar

**Tex-Mex style:** melted queso con chiles

**BLT style:** cooked bacon strips, lettuce, tomato, and mayonnaise

**Gooey-sweet style:** melted Brie cheese and brown sugar

**Hawaiian style:** pineapple ring and drizzle of teriyaki sauce

*use a small amount of each ingredient to flavor burger, but not make it too chunky

These are fun, pretty, and tasty. . . all stuck together on one stick!

## PLAN AHEAD!

The steak in this recipe needs to marinate for at least 1 hour and up to 1 day, so plan to make the marinade and let the steak soak up the good flavor.

### INGREDIENTS FOR THE MARINADE:

- ¼ cup soy sauce
- 2 tablespoons lemon juice
- 2 tablespoons brown sugar
- 2 cloves garlic, minced
- ¼ teaspoon ground ginger
- 1 20-ounce can of pineapple chunks, juices reserved

### INGREDIENTS FOR THE KEBABS:

- 2 pounds steak (London broil works great)
- 1 large green bell pepper
- 1 large red bell pepper
- 1 large sweet white onion

## Prepare marinade & steak:

1. In the mixing bowl, whisk together the soy sauce, lemon juice, brown sugar, garlic, ginger, and the reserved pineapple juice. Be sure to save the pineapple chunks for later.

2. Cut the steak into 1-inch cubes and add to the mixing bowl with the marinade. Cover with foil and put in refrigerator for at least 1 hour and up to 1 day. The longer it sits, the more flavorful it will become.

### Tools:

- Measuring cups & spoons
- Large mixing bowl
- Whisk
- Can opener
- Knife
- Cutting board
- Foil
- Small 1½-2 inch fun-shaped cookie cutter
- 8 wooden or metal skewers

## PREPARE & ASSEMBLE KEBABS:

1. Wash and dry bell peppers and onion. Make a slice on one side of the bell peppers, pull out the center and seeds and lay it flat on the cutting board. Cut the ends off the onion and pull off any outer skin. Make a slice on one side of the onion, pull off several layers, and lay them flat on the cutting board.
   Use the small cookie cutter to cut out fun veggie shapes.

2. Assemble kebabs by alternating meat, pineapple chunks, and veggie cut-outs on the skewers. Make them colorful!

3. Have an adult broil or grill kebabs for 4 minutes on one side, then turn and cook other side for 4 minutes. Repeat until steak is cooked to liking.

4. Serve kebabs on a nice platter in the middle of the table along with one of the other fabulous side dish recipes like Fireman Dean's Blazing Potatoes on page 45 or the Sweet Pot O' Beans on page 43.

# Super Spud Supper

Fill up on the simple things in life, like good old-fashioned baked potatoes!

## INGREDIENTS:
4 large russet potatoes

## TOOLS:
◆ Knife

## STEPS:
1. Preheat oven to 400°F.
2. Scrub the outside of the potatoes and bake in oven for 1 hour until tender inside.
3. While baking, decide on which stuffers you like and prepare them as noted. Slice open baked potatoes and fill 'em up!

## Spud Stuffers
◆ Chopped broccoli, olives, peppers, green onions, mushrooms, or other crunchy veggies
◆ Crumbled cooked bacon or bacon bits
◆ Butter, sour cream, cottage cheese
◆ Grated Cheese, melted cheese, crumbled feta, or other flavored cheese
◆ Chili, pesto, salsa
◆ Fresh finely chopped herbs, salt, and pepper

# Crock Pot Pork BBQ

Here's a recipe for all you little leaguers, soccer players, dancers, or just plain active kids. When you use a crock-pot, a great meal can be waiting for you at the end of a busy day.

## PLAN AHEAD!

This is a crock-pot recipe, so have everything ready the night before. In the morning you can just toss in the ingredients, turn it on, and go.

### TOOLS:

- Knife
- Crock-pot
- Salad bowl
- Spoon
- Baking sheet
- Large fork or metal tongs

### INGREDIENTS:

2-3 pound boneless pork roast
1 large white onion
1 bottle BBQ sauce
8 hamburger buns
1 package of coleslaw salad mix
1 bottle coleslaw or Ranch dressing

## In the Morning:

1. Chop white onion in small pieces and put in crock-pot.
2. Put pork roast on top of onions.

3. Pour entire bottle of BBQ sauce over the top. Cover crock-pot and set on low to allow for at least 8 hours of cooking time.

## Right Before Dinner:

1. Put coleslaw salad in salad bowl. Add dressing to taste and mix well.
2. Turn oven on low and lightly toast hamburger buns.
3. Use a large fork or metal tongs to pull the cooked pork off and generously pile on each toasted hamburger bun. Serve with coleslaw.

# Chow Down Bread Bowl Chili

Here's a hearty meal for hungry kids that's ready to eat (the bowl too!) when you get home.

## ⏰ PLAN AHEAD!

This is a crock-pot recipe, so have everything ready the night before. In the morning you can just toss in the ingredients, turn it on, and go.

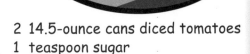

## INGREDIENTS:

- 2 pounds stew beef, cut into 1-inch cubes
- 2 teaspoons chili powder
- 1 teaspoon garlic powder
- 1 large onion, diced
- 1 large green bell pepper, seeded and diced
- 2 15-ounce cans of black beans, drained
- 2 14.5-ounce cans diced tomatoes
- 1 teaspoon sugar
- 1 6-ounce can of tomato paste
- Salt and pepper, to taste
- Round loaf of bread (found in bread/bakery section of the grocery store)
- Sour cream
- Shredded cheddar cheese

## Steps:

1. Turn the crock-pot on low and layer in the following in order:
   - ❖ 1-inch beef cubes
   - ❖ Chili and garlic powder
   - ❖ Diced onion and bell pepper
   - ❖ Drained black beans
   - ❖ Tomatoes
   - ❖ Sugar
2. Cover and cook on low for 8 to 10 hours.

## Serve It Up!

1. Preheat oven to 350°F.
2. Prepare bread bowls: Use the serrated knife to cut about 1-inch of the top of each bread bowl off. Pull out the insides of the bottom of the bread to create a bowl. Save the insides to dip into the chili. Put the bread bowls and lids on a baking sheet and bake for about 10 minutes or until lightly toasted.
3. While the bowls are toasting, open the tomato paste and stir into crock-pot along with salt and pepper to taste.
4. Ladle chili into warm bread bowls. Serve with sour cream and shredded cheddar cheese. YUM!

## Tools:

- ◆ Measuring spoons
- ◆ Crock-pot
- ◆ Paring knife
- ◆ Cutting board
- ◆ Can opener
- ◆ Serrated knife
- ◆ Baking sheet
- ◆ Ladle

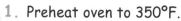

# Potato Chips Fish N' Chips

Chips ahoy, matey! These salty treasures are much better made fresh!

## INGREDIENTS:

- 1 pound fresh, boneless white fish fillets like halibut or cod
- 1 cup potato chips, crushed
- $\frac{1}{3}$ cup flour
- Seasoning of choice (salt, pepper, Italian flavoring, garlic or onion salt)
- 1 egg, slightly beaten
- $\frac{1}{4}$ cup milk
- 4 medium baking potatoes
- 1 cup dry breadcrumbs

## TOOLS:

- Cutting board
- Knife
- 3 bowls
- Whisk
- 2 baking sheets
- Mixing bowl
- 1 large zipper lock plastic bag

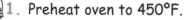

## Prep Potato Chip Fish:

1. Preheat oven to 450°F.
2. Cut fish filets into 3-inch strips.
3. Place crushed potato chips and flour in two separate bowls. Add seasoning of choice to taste to the potato chips.
4. Whisk the egg and milk in another bowl.
5. Dip fish strips in flour and shake off excess. Then dip them in milk/egg mixture. Coat with potato chips. Place coated fish strips on greased baking sheet.

## Prep Chips:

1. Wash each potato and cut into wedges. Put into mixing bowl. Add water to cover. Let soak for five minutes. Drain. Pat dry.
2. Put breadcrumbs and more seasoning into a large, zipper lock sandwich bag.
3. Place potato wedges into bag a couple at a time, seal, and shake to coat. Arrange potatoes in a single layer on greased baking sheet. Bake fish for 8-12 minutes or until crispy. Bake chips for about 15 minutes or until crispy.

### Dip Into:
 ❖ Cocktail sauce    ❖ Tartar sauce

# San Diego Finest Fish Tacos

Kids Cooking Club began in San Diego, California, which is known as "America's Finest City". Being so close to the Mexican border, one of the most popular dishes in town is fish tacos. We hope you'll find them just fine!

## INGREDIENTS:

- 1 pound fresh, mild-flavored boneless fish like halibut, shark, or red snapper
- Favorite salsa
- 1 lime
- Salt and pepper, to taste
- 12 white corn tortillas or small "home-style" flour tortillas
- 2 cups grated Monterey Jack cheese
- 1 package of coleslaw salad mix

- ½ cup mayonnaise
- ½ cup plain yogurt
- Sour cream
- 1 avocado, sliced

## TOOLS:

- ◆ Small bowl
- ◆ Fork
- ◆ Cutting board
- ◆ Knife
- ◆ Mixing bowl
- ◆ Clean dishtowel
- ◆ Foil

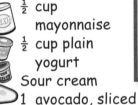

## STEPS:

1. Mix together the mayonnaise and yogurt with a fork to make a white sauce. Put in the refrigerator to chill while preparing other items.

2. Cut the fish into pieces that are about 3-inches long and 1-inch thick and put them in mixing bowl. Cut open the lime and squeeze the juice over the fish. Add several spoonfuls of salsa and salt and pepper to taste.

3. Grill or broil the fish until cooked through, about 3-5 minutes per side.

4. Wrap the tortillas in the clean kitchen towel and microwave in batches until hot, then wrap in foil to stay warm.

5. Assemble the tacos as follows:

   ❖ Warm tortilla
   ❖ Cooked fish pieces
   ❖ Sprinkle of shredded jack cheese
   ❖ Small handful of coleslaw
   ❖ Drizzle of white sauce
   ❖ Top with spoonful of salsa, sour cream, and avocado slices

Muy Bueno!

# The Big BBQ-Chicken Fish Pizza

SERVES 2 OR 4 AS AN APPETIZER

No, we aren't using fish on pizza! Actually, its one big, sweet BBQ chicken pizza shaped like a fish!

## INGREDIENTS:

2 cups cooked, boneless chicken breast, cubed
1 bottle favorite sweet BBQ sauce
1 refrigerated, pre-made pizza dough roll
Extra flour for dusting
Olive oil
1 green zucchini, thinly sliced
¼ small sweet red onion, thinly sliced
2 green onion stalks
1 cup favorite shredded, smoked cheese, like mozzarella, Gouda, or Fontina
1 olive

## TOOLS:

◆ Microwave safe bowl
◆ Spoon
◆ Cutting board
◆ Rolling pin
◆ Knife
◆ Baking sheet, greased
◆ Pastry brush

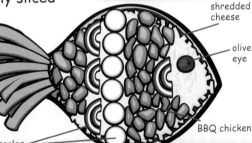

shredded cheese

olive eye

green scallion tail

BBQ chicken

zucchini & red onion scales

## STEPS:

1. Preheat oven to 425°F.

2. Place cooked cubed chicken in microwave safe bowl. Coat with sweet flavored BBQ sauce and cook for 1 minute in microwave. Set aside to cool.

3. Dust a flat work surface with flour and roll out pizza dough into a large oval shape. Cut out a large fish shape. Place on greased baking sheet. Lightly brush a thin layer of olive oil on the fish crust and bake in the oven for 5 minutes until light brown. Take out of oven and turn crust over, so baked side is on the bottom. Spread a thin layer of BBQ sauce on the top.

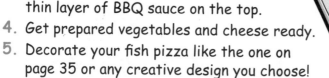

4. Get prepared vegetables and cheese ready.

5. Decorate your fish pizza like the one on page 35 or any creative design you choose!

6. Bake for 20-30 minutes until crust and toppings are crunchy and cheese is bubbly.

# Little Piggy Pot Pies

*♪ These little piggies were made from the market.*
*These little piggies were made at home.*
*These little piggies were made of chicken*
*(not roast beef).* ♪♪♫
*These little piggies had peas and carrots*
*And these little piggies said, "Wee, wee, wee,"*
*all the way down!* ♫?♪

## TOOLS:
- Knife
- Cutting board
- Mixing bowl
- 3 mini pie pans (5-inch diameter)
- Bottle cap
- Fork
- Straw
- Pastry brush
- Foil

## INGREDIENTS:
2 large, cooked, boneless chicken breasts
6 mushrooms
10.75 ounce can cream of chicken soup
3 tablespoons evaporated skim milk
½ teaspoon dried thyme
1 cup frozen peas and carrots
1 pre-made, refrigerated, "unfold and bake" piecrust to make two 9-inch pies
1 egg
1 tablespoon water

## STEPS:

1. Preheat oven to 400°F.

2. Cut chicken breasts into $\frac{1}{2}$-inch cubes. Slice mushrooms and put these and chicken in mixing bowl. Add soup, milk, thyme, carrots, and peas.

3. Lay out piecrust flat on cutting board. Use the mini pie pan and cut a circle slightly larger than the diameter of the pan. Repeat 6 times, so you have 2 dough circles for each pie. Use the bottle cap to cut 2 ears and one nose for each pie (9 round circles in all.)

4. Place one dough circle in the bottom of each pie pan. Ladle chicken/soup mixture to $\frac{2}{3}$ full. Put top circle on use fork to press down and join the circles together. Place the small round circles as ears and nose on top to make a pig's face. Use the straw to cut out nostrils and eyes.

5. Beat together the egg and water to make an egg wash. Brush on top of piggy pies with pastry brush. Bake for 15-20 minutes or until top is golden brown.

38

# Macaroni Alfredo

Serve this with garlic bread (see page 42) for an easy mid-week meal.

## INGREDIENTS:

12 ounces of elbow macaroni
$\frac{1}{2}$ cup unsalted butter
$1\frac{1}{2}$ cups heavy cream
$1\frac{1}{2}$ cups fresh grated Parmesan cheese

## TOOLS:

◆ Large pot
◆ Colander
◆ Small saucepan
◆ Slotted spoon
◆ 9-inch square baking dish

## STEPS:

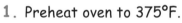

1. Preheat oven to 375°F.

2. Bring pot of water and a pinch of salt to boil over high heat. Add macaroni and cook until al dente or about 5-7 minutes. Drain macaroni in colander and put in baking dish.

3. Melt butter in small saucepan. Add cream and cheese and cook for 5 minutes, stirring continuously. Toss sauce with macaroni and bake for 20 minutes until bubbly.

# Garlic Bread

## INGREDIENTS:

1 loaf sourdough bread
1 stick unsalted butter
½ cup fresh grated Parmesan cheese
2 teaspoons minced garlic cloves

## STEPS:

1. Preheat oven to 350°F.
2. Melt the butter in the microwave. Add the Parmesan cheese and minced garlic.
3. Cut open the loaf of sourdough with serrated knife and place on baking sheet.
4. Spread flavored butter evenly on both halves. Bake for 15-20 minutes or until golden brown and bubbly.

**SERVES 6**

## TOOLS:

◆ Microwave safe bowl
◆ Serrated knife
◆ Baking sheet
◆ Pastry brush

# Sweet Pot O' Beans

The three different types of beans make this a flavorful side dish for any meal.

SERVES 8

**TOOLS:**

- Skillet
- Metal tongs
- Can opener
- Knife
- Large pot
- Slotted spoon

## INGREDIENTS:

5-6 bacon strips
1 15-ounce can of baked beans
1 15-ounce can of pinto beans, drained
1 15-ounce can of great northern white beans, drained
1 cup brown sugar
1 tablespoon Dijon mustard
½ sweet white onion, diced

## Steps:

1. Put bacon strips in skillet and cook until crunchy, turning several times. Put cooked bacon on several paper towels to absorb the fat. Cool and chop into small pieces.

2. Open cans of beans. Drain the pinto and great northern white beans and put in pot on stove. Put entire contents of baked beans in pot.

3. Add the brown sugar, Dijon mustard, and diced onion to beans and bring to a quick boil, then turn on low and let beans simmer for at least $\frac{1}{2}$ hour and up to 2-3 hours. The longer the beans simmer, the more the flavors meld together.

# Fireman Dean's Blazing Potatoes

Did you know that many firefighters are good cooks? It's because they have the responsibility of cooking for the firehouse when they are on duty 24 hours a day. One of our favorite firemen created this colorful dish and we think you'll agree that it is HOT!

## TOOLS:

◆ Cutting board
◆ Knife
◆ Large mixing bowl
◆ Slotted spoon
◆ 9 x 13-inch baking dish

## INGREDIENTS:

2 red potatoes
2 Yukon gold potatoes
2 sweet potatoes
4 any other color/kind of potato
Olive oil
Montréal steak seasoning
   (found in small jar in spice section
   of grocery store)

## STEPS:

1. Preheat oven to 375°F.

2. Wash and dry potatoes. Cut the potatoes into any shape you choose, chunked, sliced, or whatever, but just try to keep them to a good size, not too small.

3. Place cut potatoes into a large mixing bowl and pour olive oil over them, just enough to coat all of the potatoes. Add generous sprinkles of Montreal steak seasoning and mix all together with slotted spoon until the potatoes are covered uniformly with olive oil and the seasoning.

4. Transfer coated potatoes to baking dish and bake for 45 minutes or until potatoes are soft and lightly brown.

REMEMBER, THE MORE DIFFERENT POTATOES YOU USE THE NICER THE DISH WILL BE. THIS IS A BIG HIT AT THE FIREHOUSE AND IS SURE TO BE IN YOUR HOME AS WELL.

**Fireman Dean**

# Great Grilled Veggies!

**VEGGIES TO TRY:**

Bell peppers—all colors (remove seeds)
Mushrooms—regular, shitake, or portabella
Onions—red, white, or green
Potatoes—Eastern, russet, or sweet
Squash—yellow or summer

**TOOLS:**
- Knife
- Grilling grid/ grate or skewers
- Metal tongs

## STEPS:

1. Wash and prepare all vegetables .

2. Brush vegetables with olive oil or melted butter. Season to taste. Try rosemary, garlic powder, and paprika, or Italian seasoning.

3. Use a non-stick grate that is put directly on grill or put veggies on skewers. For the grate, slice your veggies about $\frac{1}{2}$-inch thick. For the skewers, use 1-inch chunks so they don't fall off.

4. Grill over medium heat, turning several times using metal tongs until vegetables are streaked with brown and are tender, about 5-7 minutes per side.

# Child's Cheesecake

An adult dessert, made by a kid!

## ⏰ PLAN AHEAD!

Cheesecake needs to set in refrigerator for at least 4 hours before serving!

### Tools:
- Mixing bowl
- Electric hand mixer
- Measuring cups

**SERVES 8**

### Ingredients:
- 1 store-bought graham cracker crust
- 8 ounces cream cheese
- $\frac{1}{3}$ cup sugar
- 1 cup sour cream
- 1 teaspoon vanilla
- 1 cup whipped topping like Cool Whip
- Fresh berries of choice: strawberries, blueberries, raspberries, or combine all, washed

### Steps:

Using the hand mixer, beat cream cheese until smooth while gradually adding sugar. Blend in sour cream and vanilla. Fold in whipped topping and blend. Put into crust and garnish with fruit. Chill until set, about 4 hours.

# Snickers Delight

Now that supper has been planned, it's time to think about dessert. You will snicker in delight when you eat this!

## ⏰ PLAN AHEAD!

This pie needs to set in freezer for at least 4 hours before serving!

### TOOLS:
- Measuring cups
- Mixing bowl
- Fork
- 9-inch pie pan
- Cutting board
- Knife

### INGREDIENTS:

- 2 cup finely crushed chocolate cookie crumbs
- ½ cup coarse-chopped peanuts
- ½ cup butter, melted
- 1 quart vanilla ice cream, softened
- 10 2-ounce size Snickers bars
- ¼ cup chocolate fudge sauce
- ¼ cup caramel sauce

## Steps:

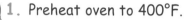

1. Preheat oven to 400°F.

2. Using a fork, mix together cookie crumbs, peanuts, and butter. Press into the bottom of pie pan and bake for 10 minutes. Let cool completely before filling.

3. While crust is baking, chop Snickers bars into small pieces.

4. Mix softened ice cream with half of the chopped candy bars and spoon into cooled crust. Drizzle with chocolate and caramel sauces and freeze for 4 hours or until set.

5. Sprinkle remaining chopped candy bars on top right before serving. Divine!

# Shirley's Simple Surprise

We named it this, because once you taste this fruitful cake, you will say, "Surely, it can't be that simple!"

## TOOLS:

- ◆ Can opener
- ◆ 9 x 13-inch baking pan
- ◆ Measuring cups
- ◆ Spatula

## INGREDIENTS:

- 1 20-ounce can crushed pineapple, opened and not drained
- 3-4 cups of frozen or fresh blueberries, blackberries, raspberries, or combination of all
- ¼ cup sugar, divided
- 1 stick butter, melted
- 1 box of yellow cake mix

1. Preheat oven to 375°F.
2. Layer the cake in the baking pan as follows:
   - ❖ Crushed pineapple along with the juices on the bottom
   - ❖ Berries of choice
   - ❖ Half of the sugar ($\frac{1}{8}$ cup)
   - ❖ Dry cake mix
   - ❖ Melted butter
   - ❖ Remaining half of the sugar ($\frac{1}{8}$ cup)

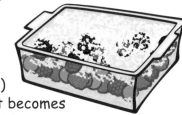

3. Bake 30-40 minutes or until top just becomes light brown and berries start to bubble.

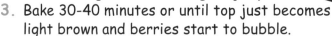

## SIMPLE SERVING IDEAS:

- ❖ Serve warm with a dollop of vanilla ice cream on top
- ❖ Serve in a tall parfait glass topped with whipped cream
- ❖ Serve with a mug of milk and dip into milk while you eat

# No Time To Bake Dessert

Try this no bake dessert in a classroom or at a scout meeting when there is not an oven available.

**SERVES 8**

## CRUST INGREDIENTS:

- ½ cup dried banana chips
- ⅓ cup dried apricots
- ⅓ cup dried pineapple
- ⅓ cup raisins
- ¼ cup orange juice

## FILLING INGREDIENTS:

- ⅓ cup dried apples
- 4 Granny Smith apples
- 2 teaspoons lemon juice
- 1 teaspoon cinnamon
- 2 tablespoons honey
- ¼ cup dried banana chips

## TOOLS:

- Measuring spoons & cups
- Food processor or blender
- Spatula
- 9-inch pie pan, greased
- Apple slicer
- Mixing bowl
- Small plastic bag

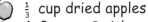

51

## STEPS:

1. In food processor or blender, add the banana chips, dried apricots, dried pineapple, raisins, and orange juice. Turn on and puree mixture into a thick pastelike crust. Press this crust into the bottom and sides of the pie pan with clean hands.

2. Place the dried apples on top of the crust.

3. Wash and core Granny Smith apples. Cut into thin slices and put in mixing bowl. Add the lemon juice, cinnamon, and honey and mix well with spatula.

4. Put apple mixture on top of dried apples.

5. Put the remaining $\frac{1}{4}$ cup dried banana chips into a small plastic bag and crush into fine pieces. Sprinkle on top of apple mixture and chill for at least $\frac{1}{2}$ hour before eating. ENJOY!

# Smashing Strawberry Pie

This should be a splendid success!

## INGREDIENTS:

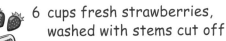

- 6 cups fresh strawberries, washed with stems cut off
- 1 cup sugar
- 3 tablespoons cornstarch
- 2 tablespoons lemon juice
- 9-inch pre-baked, deep-dish, found in freezer section of grocery store
- $\frac{1}{2}$ cup whipping cream, whipped

## TOOLS:

- ◆ Saucepan
- ◆ Potato masher
- ◆ Slotted spoon

## STEPS:

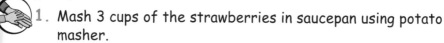

1. Mash 3 cups of the strawberries in saucepan using potato masher.

2. Add sugar and cornstarch and bring to simmer over medium heat.

3. Stir until thickened and clear, about 3-5 minutes. Mix in lemon juice. Remove from heat and let cool.

4. Save 4 whole strawberries for the top. Add remaining whole strawberries to the cooled mixture from above and spoon into crust.

5. Top with whipped cream and 4 saved strawberries. Refrigerate pie for about an hour to serve chilled.

# The Table Is Set

The best start to any good meal is the first impression it makes, and it starts with the table. Here's the layout for an informal and formal place setting. Add your own special touches like a decorative centerpiece, candles, fancy napkins, fresh flowers in a vase, or personalized place cards. Be creative and make a lasting impression!

## Informal Place Setting

## Formal Place Setting

# Remember the Good Times

The dishes have been cleared and the last dessert plate licked clean. The supper is over but the memories will live on. You will remember the time you spent together for a long time to come! Get ready to share some more fun in the kitchen.

All true chefs take good care of their kitchen and tools. Clean up after you cook and take good care of the cooking gifts in this package by hand washing and drying them after each use.

Check out www.kidscook.com for more delicious fun for everyone.